MY PET FISH

Animal Book 4-6
Children's Animal Books

In this book, we're going to cover how to choose and take care of a pet fish. So, let's get right to it!

You've asked your parents and they've said that they'll let you get a pet fish! Pet fish aren't that difficult to take care of, but there are certain things you need to do to make sure your new pet stays healthy and happy.

CHOOSING YOUR FISH

When a lot of people think of a pet fish, they think of a goldfish in a goldfish bowl. However, goldfish are not the easiest fish to take care of. Some types get quite large. Also, in almost all cases, a bowl isn't a good way to keep a fish because fish need filtered water. If they live in unfiltered water, they can die.

GUPPY

Two of the best species of fish that you could choose are guppies and platies. These fish are hardy, which just means that they don't get sick or die easily. They also don't get too large, just about 2 inches long as adults.

ome types of platies are bright red when they become adult fish. Guppies become shades of green and yellow on both their fins and bodies when they're adults. Guppies or platies are only two of the possible types you could buy.

Before you pick the fish that you think is the right pet for you, it's time to get the water at your home tested.

PLATY

GOLDFISH

WORKING WITH WATER

Certain types of fish do better in certain types of water. You'll have an easier time keeping your new pet healthy if it's the type of fish that does well in the water you already have. It's best to use your home tap water, but not all tap water is the same.

Your home water could be more acid than alkaline or it could be the opposite. It could also be soft or hard. Soft water doesn't have many chemicals dissolved in it, while hard water has a lot of chemicals in it. You'll also need to think about whether you want to have a coolwater aquarium or one that is heated.

When you measure whether your water at home is acid or alkaline, you're testing its pH level. You can get a kit to help you do this. It will have strips you can put into the water to test the pH level.

If you don't want to test the water yourself, you can take it to your local pet store and they will test it for you. If your water is acid, it's also soft water. If it's alkaline that means it has a lot of chemicals in it and it is hard water.

So, in a way, there are two different types: soft water that is acidic and hard water that is alkaline.

Once you know what type of water you have and whether you want a tank that's heated or isn't, then you have the information you need to make a choice of which type of fish would make the best pet for you. You should narrow your choice down to two or three types and then ask at the pet store.

Here are the possible combinations you could have:

- ➲ Coldwater aquarium with soft acid water
- ➲ Coldwater aquarium with hard alkaline water
- ➲ Heated aquarium with soft acid water
- ➲ Heated aquarium with hard alkaline water

You should probably start with a fresh-water aquarium or tank since saltwater tanks, also called marine tanks, take more effort.

RESEARCHING YOUR FISH

Not all fish experts agree as to which fish makes the best first pet. You and your parents should do a little bit of research before choosing the type you want. Here are some types to consider:

SPOTTED MOLLY

MOLLY FISH FROM CENTRAL AND SOUTH AMERICA

Molly fish are very colorful and for the most part they do well in a tank with other types of fish. They do best in freshwater tanks that are heated. Molly fish thrive in water that has a little salt but you can use an aquarium salt for them.

Check with your pet shop and see what they recommend. Molly fish, also called mollies, are really fun to watch since they like to play "hide and seek" in plants.

PLATY FISH FROM CENTRAL AMERICA AND MEXICO

Platy fish, also called platies or moon fish, are very peaceful fish. They are sometimes confused with goldfish since some types are a similar color. Some types are black and they come in colors of red and also blue.

They are active and fun to watch. One thing to keep in mind is that if you get more than one you may end up with lots of babies in your tank.

ANGEL FISH

ANGEL FISH FROM SOUTH AMERICA

Most people think that angel fish are quite beautiful and they are usually peaceful. When a male and female fish choose each other as mates, they mate for life and will only have baby fish with each other. They like warm water and will need a pretty big tank to be comfortable. They eat a lot of different types of food such as fish flakes and either live or frozen fish food.

GUPPIES FROM SOUTH AMERICA

Guppies are one of the most popular types of fish for pets. They are happy-go-lucky and get along with each other as well as most other types of fish. They do like having other guppies around, so if you decide to get guppies, you may want to buy more than one. The males are very colorful and the females are silvery in color. They come in almost every color of the rainbow.

GUPPY

BETTA

BETTA FISH FROM LAOS, CAMBODIA, VIETNAM, AND THAILAND

Betta fish are also called Siamese Fighting Fish and there's a reason why. If you have two males in your tank, they will more than likely fight with each other. They fight until one dies.

So, if you buy more than one fish make certain that you're only getting one male. They don't do well with other fish because they sometimes eat the baby fish of the other species. They've also been known to jump completely out of the tank so you'll need a tank cover. They do best when they're by themselves.

TIPS TO TAKE CARE OF YOUR FISH

Fish really like temperatures that stay the same. Don't place your tank near a heater or fireplace. Even direct sunlight can cause a change in temperature.

Fish are calm and don't like the vibration of a lot of noise. It might be a good idea to keep their tank away from the television set or stereo.

Sometimes your tap water can have added chlorine as well as fluoride. These may be dangerous to fish, so have your parents help you test the pH of the water when you put your fish back into their aquarium.

Fish make two different kinds of waste. One type is CO2 from their gills as they take in oxygen from the water and breathe out. The other type is poop! These wastes increase ammonia in the tank, which can kill your fish. Cleaning your tank regularly is very important.

Just like people, not all fish get along. Some fish get very upset or aggressive if other fish are in their territory, so do your research and ask the experts at the pet store for more information before putting fish together in the same tank.

Make sure you buy fish that are healthy. Healthy fish are active and clear-eyed. The fish should have clean scales with no sores on its body.

BEWARE
SHARKS

CHOOSING A TANK

You'll need to decide whether you're going to get one pet fish or a whole tank full of pets. The type of fish you choose to buy will make a difference in the size tank you choose.

Aquariums come in all different sizes from 5 gallon to 20 gallon and above. Overcrowding is a very common problem in aquariums. You want to make sure your fish have enough space to be comfortable and stay healthy.

DAILY ROUTINE FOR YOUR FISH

- Make up a chart so you don't forget the things you need to do to take care of your fish. Every day you'll need to:

- Give your fish the appropriate food.

- Get rid of any food that's been uneaten and is floating at the top of the tank water.

- Check the temperature of the water and keep a record of it.

- Let your mom or dad know if something doesn't seem OK.

Every few days you'll need to:

- ➲ Check the water to see if it's safe.
- ➲ Make sure the heater is working, if your tank has one.
- ➲ Clean out at least 1/3 of the water weekly.
- ➲ Clean out the entire tank.

IF YOUR FISH DIES

It's really sad when you get attached to your pet and it dies. This can happen for a lot of reasons. Just learn from the experience and make sure that you're keeping your tank clean and checking the water to make sure that it's safe.

Awesome! Now you know more about how to take care of your new pet fish. You can find more Animal books from Baby Professor by searching the website of your favorite book retailer.

Visit

BABY PROFESSOR
EDUCATION KIDS

www.BabyProfessorBooks.com
to download Free Baby Professor eBooks
and view our catalog of new and exciting
Children's Books